Also by

Verna Gillis

I JUST WANT TO BE INVITED – I Promise Not to Come (Life as One-Liners)

This book is a work of non fiction. All and any references are to real people or as real as these people are.

Copyright 2015

Translated from the psychological emotional delusional dysfunctional aspirational

Cover photo: Eva Tenuto

I'LL NEVER KNOW IF I WOULD HAVE
GOTTEN THE SAME RESULTS
IF I'D BEEN NICE

TERROR FIRMA

"It's all good."
Really?
It's not all good.
Haven't you noticed?

Jewish mysticism:
Why did my mother treat me like that?

"I Remember Trauma"
the family story – no names, no blame,
no shame – just what happened.

I always knew I was home-ophobic!

Any old business?
Here I am!

Irony pills – take several daily
to keep your perspective well toned!

There are outies and there are innies –
the over reactors and the over withholders

Emotionally starved and physically stuffed, I cut loose from the mother ship and floated out there alone with my eating disorder.

I was the only person I knew who could eat on cocaine.

When you don't get what you need,
you want what you want.

My bottom line addiction is to feeling bad.

My fault lines are still active.

I was born an anxiety addict in utero from my mother directly to me.

Hypochondriacs get it right.
There is something wrong.

Just not what we thought.

I am working on a new app called
SHOULD I SHIT MYSELF?
You input information about a relationship, job, strange-looking animal in your path.

The app will either give you an **OK**, thumbs up! or **SHIT YOURSELF**, which is a danger sign few people actually ever heed.

As a Girl Scout the three badges I could have earned most easily were stealing, overeating, and lying.

"I married your mother, but you will have to marry a perfect stranger!"
-- Ivan Gillis

I was never one of those people
who "fell in love."
I always described it as being clitorized.

The entitled and the disenfranchised will find each other and fall madly in love.

We are all operating
under gross mythconceptions.

Are Jews good or bad for the Jews?

You can always trust me to be myself.

Gluten: Bring it on!

Lactose Tolerant

I never had children,
and the children I never had are grateful.

4 Stages of Comedy:

Stand Up

Sit Down

Recline

Lie Down
(for the final act)

"For those nervy types who need to relax, come recharge your brash behavior at the ChutzSpa."
-- David Gillis

I am a personal expert on taking my partner hostage, also known as a road trip!

Wouldn't you prefer to be with someone who has already bottomed out?

The only commandments I have
not broken are:
I have not killed; nor have I
coveted my neighbor's wife.

Paradox Lost

Paradox Found

Paradox Reigns

I keep a journal which I call
WHAT I DID NOT SAY TODAY!

What a relief not feeling like
the only sick fuck in the room.

Shame-onism -- a soul destroying ritual of self- incrimination filled with malevolent spirits of self-doubt where our sick secrets thrive.

I gave too much of myself nurturing fabricated connections and never got a seat at the table.

I'm a groan up.

Don't think about anything.
No good came come from it.

We all do the best we can.
For some that is better than others.
Best in show!

One of the best relationships I have had
in my life has been with scones,
and I am here to tell you:
It is better to have sconed and lost than
never to have sconed at all.

My Way – The Right Way: A Guide to Unfulfillment.

BOOK OF RANTS:
Rants for all occasions. Prize-winning rants; new up-and-coming rant writers - expand your repertoire of rants so as not to bore the rantee. S(he) will be impressed by your wide range of approaches to verbal decimation and the creative way in which you assure that no change will occur or be possible. Lock in your victim. Rants to help you in unexpected ways!

INSULTS OF LAST RESORT:
Hitting below the emotional belt

We choose people who help us keep the
safe barrier safe, meaning
not too close for discomfort.

"You can't reason with a rooster."
-- Jake Berthot

What didn't I do to deserve this?

We all have to live with each other's imperfections or exist in solitary confinement.

"The average person is way below average."
-- Ivan Gillis

I finally found my voice.
Before that I had my scream, my shriek.

The random sperm theory of life:
One gets through and people try
to build a life on that.
Think about it!

The all-or-nothing scenario --
but all of nothing has nothing to offer,
and some of something is,
more often than not, good enough.

I don't know what's best for me,
but I always know what is best for my partner.

Game show idea
YOUR CALL IS VERY IMPORTANT TO US!
Five contestants.
Each contestant is given the same
800 number to call.
The person who gets to speak to a real,
live human first, wins.

Introducing a new service:
Ragers for Hire –
with a bulldog determination and a bad pit bull gene we will get you results dealing with the corporate time suckers mother fuckers known as banks and financial institutions.

Promise-cuity:
The addictive habit of promising over and over what one cannot possibly promise.

HOW TO SURVIVE FIDELITY IN MARRIAGE:

Have affairs!
Many affairs succeed because both are married to other people.
Many marriages last because one or both have affairs.

"There's always a backdrop of residual tzuris."
-- Danny Louis

I was a catastrophizer.

Find as many ways as possible to disassociate!
Keep a tool box of dissociative techniques
nearby at all times.

"I'm just coping with infinity."
-- Roswell Rudd

If looks could kill I would have been mortally wounded.

I have an opinion about every - fucking - thing – including the way my partner tells stories about his own life! I tell them better of course.

When you think you've found your soul mate, and it feels so cozy and familiar –
Run the other way.
You are now ready for the family re-enactment.
Enter – two innocents.

I worry if I'm worrying
about the right things.

If they annulled gay marriage
there would have been a class action
by straight people for equal rights.

I'm neither as nice nor as bad as I thought!

"I wish I didn't understand."
-- Renee Gillis

I often sit in toxic silence not saying shit but thinking it.

"You continue to cease to amaze me."
  -- Michael Doucet

Some people lament their imperfections.
I strive for imperfection.
It would be a big step up
from being totally whacked.

I'll never know if I would have gotten the same results if I had been nice.

That person dreads seeing me.
I dread seeing that person's dread of me.
Dread-locked.

I have visitations of myself.
Demons on parade here –
nightly in Kerhonkson.

I need a psychopractor for those daily attitude adjustments.

Give me an example of doing nothing.
Seriously.
Who has ever experienced it?

The 4 Stages of Life
Rock n' Drool
Rock n' Roll
Rock n' Drole
Rock n' Drool

I was always spinning a sad yearn.

"I'm on a not need to know basis."
-- Rolf Sturm

Terror firma.

The certitude of the great uncertainty
is more certain.

I'm in the infancy of older.

Don't let anything leave you breathless.

The difference between life and death is breath.

Sometimes it *is* too late.

I'm on the road to total incontinence.

Musical chairs is really preparing us for death.

My compassion for some people is in direct
proportion to my distance from them;
the greater the distance,
the greater my compassion.

Dying is the ultimate out-of-body experience.

Top o' the mournin' to you!

I've had it with the Holocaust.

"Put me out of your misery."
-- Aram Rubenstein-Gillis

The show can't always go on.

Thank you for the ears and hearts of the dear people in my life to whom I can talk openly and honestly – and most dear Roswell who, living with me, may be experiencing some of the benefits of ensuing hard of hearingness!

With increasing awareness of the deepest love and gratitude for my parents. Having survived being their daughter and having survived myself, I can focus on the gifts.

They both shared great liberal values – any one was welcome in our home.

My father, Ivan Gillis, was the first very funny person in my life. His humor kept the family going. He instilled in all of us the concept of greatness – that it exists and manifests through people in what they create, how they behave, and what they can accomplish.

We grew up with "culture heroes" running the gamut from Paul Robeson, Marian Anderson, FDR, Toscanini, Babe Ruth, Mickey Mantle, Arthur Rubenstein, Jascha Heifetz, Vladimir Horowitz, Tom Lehrer, Elaine May & Mike Nichols, Edward R Murrow - the soundscape of our childhood.

I continued to find new culture heroes. That appreciation became my quest, and I discovered what I could do working with some very great talents. My life put me in the middle of music and creativity.

My mother, Freda Nieburg Gillis, M.D., was a powerful example of a modern, professional and free thinking woman. She encouraged and supported me to do and pursue in the world, as she had done. She was warm, empathetic, kind and had great capacity for a wide range of people. When she was good mommy, she really was.

Thank you to Linda Fite for her superb editing skills and numerous other talents applied for the betterment of this endeavor.

Thank you to Alex Trimpe for his creative design skills and ideas and funny emails.

And just to name some names - david renee ivan aram sarah max ezri jonah tova kyla and the greater tribal family – you know who you are.

Kerhonkson, May 12, 2015

www.ingramcontent.com/pod-product-compliance
Lightning Source LLC
Chambersburg PA
CBHW032149040426
42449CB00005B/450